Michael John O'Neill is a playwright, dramaturg and theatre producer from the north coast of Ireland. Michael's first play, *Akedah*, won the Bruntwood Prize Original New Voice Award 2019 and premiered in the Hampstead Theatre Downstairs in 2023. His second play *This is Paradise* was presented at Traverse Theatre in both 2021 and 2022 as part of the Edinburgh Festival Fringe and won the Popcorn Writing Award 2021. In 2020 his digital short *Sore Afraid* was produced by National Theatre of Scotland, Citizens Theatre, and BBC Scotland, and his audio short *Part of That World* was produced by Pitlochry Festival Theatre. He is developing new plays with the Almeida Theatre (as part of the Genesis New Writers' Programme), Lyric Theatre Belfast and National Theatre of Scotland (as Writer on Attachment). In 2022 he completed the BBC Voices Programme and was shortlisted for the Element Pictures Northern Irish Writers' Award. He has an original TV show in development with House Productions. His work as a theatre producer includes as Artistic Producer of the Tron Theatre (2014–2020), where he founded the Tron's new work department and commissioned and produced Isobel McArthur's *Pride & Prejudice** (**sort of*).

by the same author from Faber

THIS IS PARADISE

MICHAEL JOHN O'NEILL

Akedah

faber

First published in 2023
by Faber and Faber Limited
74–77 Great Russell Street
London WC1B 3DA

Typeset by Brighton Gray
Printed and bound in the UK by CPI Group (Ltd), Croydon CR0 4YY

A CIP record for this book
is available from the British Library

978-0-571-38344-3

2 4 6 8 10 9 7 5 3 1

Acknowledgements

This play would not be as it is now were it not for Suzanne Bell, Marina Carr, Ruby Campbell, Christina McClements, Flora Connor-Rattray, Naomi Dawson, Beth Duke, Lucianne McEvoy, Jodi Gray, Grace Hans, Dorothy Jones, Trei Keep, Phil Kelly, Mairead McKinley, Carla Langley, Lily Levinson, Hannah Lyall, Rebecca Mairs, Kei Miller, Lynsey-Anne Moffat, Amy Molloy, Lucy Morrison, Davina Moss, Kevin Murphy, Katherine Nesbitt, Iris O'Neill, Jack O'Neill, Jan O'Neill, Linden O'Neill, Rosa O'Neill, Kate Reid, Imogen Sarre, Roxana Silbert, Chloe Smith, Tessa Walker, Rob Willoughby, Dinah Wood, aran Cafe Linlithgow, British Library, Casarotto Ramsay & Associates, Causeway Coast Vineyard, Creative Scotland, Faber, Hampstead Theatre, Linlithgow Library, London North Eastern Railway, Portstewart Library, Student Theatre at Glasgow, The Arches, the Peggy Ramsay Foundation, Traverse Theatre, and anonymous readers at Abbey Theatre, Bruntwood Prize, National Theatre of Scotland, Papatango Prize, Playwrights' Studio Scotland, Royal Court, Soho Theatre, Theatre503.

Akedah was first performed at Hampstead Theatre, London, on 10 February 2023, with the following cast:

Kelly Ruby Campbell
Sarah Mairead McKinley
Gill Amy Molloy

Director Lucy Morrison
Designer Naomi Dawson
Lighting Kevin Murphy
Sound Beth Duke

for Jan

Characters

Gill
thirty-three

Kelly
eighteen

Sarah
fifty-two

AKEDAH

The vastness of space. The noise of everything. Gill is illuminated. She is dressed like she is going for a job interview at an estate agent's. She is soaked through and shivering. She clenches a bursting set of keys in one hand. Her eyes are closed and she is making a low hum. A foot stamp. A yelp. A big dirty sneeze.

Gill Here I am. You says the word. And here I am so I am so I am.

Gill hums.

Awk it's no bother. No no no no no. No bother at all.

Gill hums. She is growing frustrated.

Speak to me. Please, baby. Speak.

Gill's hum is splitting apart the bones in her face.

Always our deal. Since the beginning of the beginning. You says the word, I come running. So say it. Say. It. Say anything, just, don't, stop that, don't turn away from me again –

Deep within the noise of everything, Gill hears a phone ringing. She grips her set of keys tightly.

No.

Gill shakes her head.

Hm hm, no.

The ringing gets louder.

Away, no, away now, go away.

The ringing stops. We hear heavy breathing down the phone line. Gill opens one eye. She surveys her surroundings. She holds her keys out defensively. She closes both eyes again. She laughs. Her voice becomes lower and gruffer. It is both live and pre-recorded, layering in on top of itself.

(*Smiling.*) No no no no no. You won't get me like that.

Gill swipes the keys in front of her.

Cheeky betch.

Gill swipes the keys in front of her.

(*Some anger.*) Enough. Gillian. There's work needs doing. Sure if not you, then who else? (*Beat.*) Ahhh, there she is, always my wee loyal girl, my wee prize fighter . . . sure don't you scrub up well. We should put you on front of house more often. Gorgeous. He's a lucky man so he is. (*Loud, sudden.*) Yeo!

Lights up. Kelly has appeared. She is wearing a wetsuit, and over that a T-shirt with a simple design featuring the words 'Welcome Home'. In her reality she has entered the room to find Gill stood still, staring into nothing, lost in a dwam. Gill jabs at Kelly's gut with her key fist, but Kelly catches Gill's hand. It takes some force from Kelly to stop Gill from pushing the key into her.

Kelly Hai, hai, Gill. It's me. It's Kelly.

Gill opens her eyes. She is disorientated. She sees her hand holding the keys out, straining to reach Kelly. Gill is puzzled by this, as if her hand has nothing to do with her. Confusion gives way to horror. Gill lets go of the keys. Kelly lets go of Gill's arm.

The full room is illuminated now. It is an anteroom next to a huge auditorium where Christian worship happens. The room overlooks the beach and the Atlantic

4

*Ocean, with two sides of the space entirely walled by
floor-to-ceiling glass panels.*

  *On the back wall is a graphic that reads 'Give HIM
Thanks'. Otherwise the room is clean, uncluttered, cosy.
Above them hangs a light fixture. At certain points in the
action, when Gill feels the noise of everything most
acutely, these lights will flicker and blare in sympathy
with her distress.*

(*Cheerfully admonishing.*) Have you gone doolally, woman?

  *Kelly moves to the entrance and picks up a sports bag.
She moves back to Gill and drops the bag in front of her.*

Jeepers creepers. Dry clothes in there. Hoody, joggers.
Washed of course. You'll not be reeking of me. (*Laughs.*)
I can't believe you're here, it's been so long –

  Kelly moves towards Gill to embrace her. Gill flinches.

Gill (*quiet*) Ask first.

  Kelly stops.

Kelly Yes, or course. I forgot. (*Beat.*) Clothes in the bag.

  *Kelly goes to the window and looks down. She is relieved
to see activity on the beach.*

Looks like they're back to it down there. So nothing to
worry about, if that's what's eating you . . . no fatalities.

  Kelly laughs.

Did you see much on the way up from the beach? I was
rushing you, I'm sorry. I could show you around properly,
would you like that? (*Beat.*) Have you had a look out these
windows yet? Come on and look.

  Gill doesn't move.

You can see the whole beach. And that ocean, Gill . . .

Kelly sighs with admiration.

On a clear day, you can see Scotland. (*Deep breath.*) Being up here, this view. Makes me feel lifted, stronger, you know? Seeing that.

Gill (*disengaged*) Seeing Scotland?

Kelly No. God's majesty. (*Beat.*) Oh and here, Gill, see what I can do with this phone, it's class . . .

Kelly goes to the bag. She rummages inside.

(*Mock surprise.*) Oh wait. Stop all the clocks. Who's this?

Kelly hums the third movement Chopin's Piano Sonata No. 2 (the Funeral March) and pulls a large baby sheep soft toy out of the bag. She solemnly puppeteers it in front of Gill. Gill doesn't engage.

(*Sheep voice.*) Gill . . . Gill . . . Give me a kiss. I won't eat your lips. Promise. (*Normal voice.*) Deadsheep, how'd you get in here? You remember this cheeky wee zombie don't you Gill? (*Sheep voice.*) Kiss kiss, chomp chomp.

Kelly places Deadsheep on a chair and then pretends like it falls to the ground.

Oh my word!

Kelly puts Deadsheep back in position on the chair.

Sorry. Sorry. There you are. There you go. You sit here and be good. (*Sheep voice.*) No.

Kelly laughs. She goes back to the bag. She pulls out her phone.

Aye, anyway, before we were rudely interrupted . . . this is incredible Gill, wait and see. (*Confidently.*) You want some choons?

Kelly holds the phone receiver close to her mouth. She presses a button. The phone emits a tone that indicates it is listening for instruction.

Please play the playlist 'Christian bangers'.

Kelly indicates broadly to the room and nods at Gill.

Now, listen (*Beat.*) it's good, all chart stuff, R&B, not worship. (*Beat.*) It's good. (*Beat.*) Takes a minute.

Kelly holds the phone to her mouth again.

Please play 'Christian bangers' –

Phone I'm having trouble connecting –

Kelly 'Christian bangers' –

Phone I'm having trouble connecting.

Kelly Please play 'Christian bangers' –

The phone emits an unhappy tone.

Sometimes it does this.

Kelly crosses Gill and slips the phone back into her bag.

But if it was working, the sound . . . Gill . . . It's huge, it comes from everywhere.

Gill (*with some effort*) Why am I here?

Kelly After what happened down there in the water . . . I needed . . . I thought it would be better to go somewhere private –

Gill (*sharp*) No.

Gill focuses herself.

Why am I here?

Kelly isn't sure she understands. She carries on regardless.

Kelly What you did . . .

This is like a bucket of cold water in Gill's face, her attention snaps to Kelly.

Gill What I did?

Kelly You didn't have to do that. It isn't what you think.

Kelly's phone starts ringing.

Houl on Gill.

Kelly goes to get the phone from the bag again but Gill grabs it first. Kelly tries to take it back, but Gill knocks her hand away. She instinctively uses more force than is necessary.

Gill Don't snatch.

Kelly rubs her injured hand.

Kelly It'll be them.

Gill lets the phone ring in her hand.

If I don't answer they're going to come looking for me. Is that what you want?

Gill considers this. She hands the phone to Kelly. Kelly answers.

Hiya. How is she? You're sure, no need for stitches? (*Beat.*) Okay, thank goodness. (*Beat.*) I know, thank you. (*Beat.*) Give her a big hug from me. (*Beat.*) Thank you.

Kelly looks at Gill.

Aye, oh aye, all fine.

Kelly interrupts the person on the phone.

(*Whispered.*) I'm with the lady now. (*Beat.*) That's alright. Have you spoke to Richard? (*Beat.*) Speak to Richard. (*Beat.*) No.

Kelly walks to the window and waves down.

Here, do you see me? Next to the worship hall, in . . . Aye, that's right, there we are, hiya.

Kelly laughs. Gill, investigating her surroundings, starts moving towards the exit.

Goodness gracious, it's looking lively down there now. (*To Gill.*) Where are you going?

Gill ignores her.

(*To the phone.*) No, sorry . . . (*To Gill.*) Stop, not out there. Not without me.

Gill stays where she is.

(*To the phone.*) You'd like to come up?

Gill shakes her head and waves a hand to say no.

No, I think we're more comfortable it being just the two of us.

Gill moves back into the room. Kelly's expression shifts. She turns away from Gill.

Uh-huh. (*Beat.*) Of course. (*Beat.*) Of course. Only when she's ready.

Kelly thinks for a moment about where to put her phone. She puts it on the seat next to Deadsheep.

(*To Gill.*) Don't let me forget that. Forever losing it I am.

Gill She okay then?

Kelly doesn't know how she should respond.

That woman in the water.

Kelly The woman.

Gill (*sharp*) Is there an echo in here? (*Beat.*) Were you not just talking about her . . . That wee granny who you were hiding under the waves. Gave me a fright so she did.

Kelly (*cautiously*) Oh.

Gill Fucking beast from below. (*Laughs.*) Christ I'm awful. Clumsy bitch. Fell into her.

Kelly You fell into her.

Gill There's that echo again. Thought it was just you and that fella there, splashing about. And then she popped out from underneath. Shat my knickers.

Kelly It was her baptism.

Gill Oh was it? She looked a bit long in the tooth for all that.

Kelly I don't know, if you think about it, age God must be now, we're all weans to Him.

Gill laughs. Kelly doesn't.

Gill Right . . .

Kelly You didn't recognise her?

Gill Who . . . The granny? Should I have recognised her?

Kelly No . . . Just . . . the way you came running into the water –

Gill I was . . . confused –

Kelly You came right at her.

Gill Fuck off. No I didn't. I told you I didn't see her. I was coming for you. (*Beat.*) I thought . . . I thought I might've maybe caught her with my keys.

Kelly You did.

Gill Oh Christ.

Kelly But she's fine. A bit shaken. A wee cut here . . .

Kelly touches her temple.

it wasn't bleeding loads –

Gill Oh Christ.

Kelly But she's fine now, really. That's what they were saying, on the phone, just a sticky plaster job.

Gill Thank fuck for that. (*Laughs.*) Lucky escape! (*Serious.*) No police?

Kelly No.

Gill Good. Good. (*Smiles.*) First time meeting all these new friends of yours. Hate to get a reputation for going about cutting up wee grannies.

Kelly Here comes Kelly's sister the granny-stabber . . . Especially when you've only ever stabbed this one granny.

Gill As far as you know.

Kelly Oh my goodness, yes . . . I never even thought, all these years away

The remark about it having been years sits uneasily with Gill.

you could have been all across the world leaving a trail of stabbed grannies. Lots of wee oul bodies strewn out there, all full of holes.

Gill Holy grannies.

Kelly looks at Gill blankly. It takes a beat for the pun to land.

Kelly (*cheerful*) Oh, good one.

Beat.

Gill You saying them people knew me as your sister?

Kelly (*quickly*) No.

Gill You says Kelly's sister. Kelly's sister who stabs grannies.

Kelly Joking.

Gill Are you sure about that?

Kelly I never talk about you.

Gill Good. Don't like people thinking they know me.

Kelly I remember.

Gill Tell me about the fella.

Kelly What fella?

Gill Your splashy friend in the water –

Kelly You're talking about him who helped you –

Gill Pushed me.

Kelly No he didn't –

Gill He was rough with me.

Kelly (*cheerful*) You wanting sympathy now –

Gill He was rough with me.

Kelly Gill . . . you weren't acting right.

Gill Who is he?

Kelly His name is Richard. He's senior pastor.

Gill He's what?

Kelly He's in charge.

Gill In charge of what? (*Beat.*) In charge of you?

Kelly You ran into the water screaming at us –

Gill (*incredulous*) Now houl on a minute, I was not screaming.

Kelly Aye you were.

Gill That's . . . That's revisionist so it is. That's you changing things out of badness. (*Beat.*) This Richard fella, he knew me.

Kelly No one round here knows you.

Gill He knew me.

Kelly He doesn't know you.

Gill He looked at me like he knew me.

Kelly That's how he looks at people.

Gill Oh aye?

Kelly He's got a friendly look.

Gill Friendly?

Kelly Very friendly. He's famous for it.

Gill I wouldn't say friendly.

Kelly Would you not?

Gill No, not friendly.

Kelly What would you say?

Gill Hungry.

Kelly Maybe he skipped breakfast.

Gill Good hairline on him.

Kelly Sure he's famous for that too.

Gill He told you something. Told you with his body close. And then he touched your backside.

Kelly He did not touch my backside, when was he touching my backside?

Gill Close enough he was touching. Like youse were courting.

Kelly You think we're boyfriend and girlfriend? (*Beat.*) No, he's not my boyfriend. He's oul and married and has one son already training to be a doctor. Goodness' sake woman. I've not heard from you in frigging years –

Gill after Daddy went –

Kelly and you're asking me this? –

13

Gill I needed a wee holiday –

Kelly Am I shifting some fella nearly got his bus pass –

Gill (*raising voice*) I'm asking you what you're doing with these happy-clappy freaks? –

Kelly – Keep it down, keep it down.

Gill What age are you now?

Kelly Eighteen.

Gill Fuck me. When did that happen?

Kelly January.

Gill Sure, well, whatever age you are –

Kelly Eighteen –

Gill Mummy was younger than you when she took up with Daddy.

Kelly Took up with him . . . Is that what she did?

Gill What else would you call it?

Kelly The grooming of a vulnerable young woman –

Gill Vulnerable! –

Kelly by a –

Gill Our mummy, a vulnerable woman. Now I've heard it all –

Kelly By a man . . .

Gill laughs.

By a man who did things –

Gill Deadsheep, are you hearing this? Our daddy, prepare yourself now . . . he was a man who did 'things'.

Kelly He was known to have connections –

Gill Watch yourself now –

Kelly Paramilitary criminal connections –

Gill It's a sin to speak ill of the dead –

Kelly Oh come on, Gill.

Gill Don't you 'come on' me. Daddy had a lot more to him than just that. A big hard belly of a man. With ambition. But softness as well, if you came at him right. Whatever you're hearing now . . . whatever stuck-up, Strand Road, Burnside types are in your fucking ear . . . they're making more of it than it was is all I'll say. Him and them boyos . . . they just liked to be seen carrying round big sticks. Liked the feel of the looks it would get them. Paramilitary . . . They fucking wished, fucking wannabe C Company –

Kelly It was more than that . . . What was expected of her . . . (*Beat.*) Gill, he was not a good man.

Gill laughs.

Gill There it is!

Kelly What?

Gill Still just a wee babby she is, going on about goodies and baddies. No idea about our mummy. Me, years under her, I can still see her clearly in the doorway there, wobbling on those five-inch heels, face dripping off her. Back in the day, ask anyone, they'll say it was fifty-fifty between her and him. (*Beat.*) And it wasn't Daddy who left you to die in a ditch.

Kelly She didn't leave me to die in a ditch.

Gill Who knows what could have happened to you? Palpitations, just thinking about it. You're lucky, age you were, you'll have no real memory.

Kelly I do –

Gill waves her hand.

Nahp. No. I have not come all this way to get reacquainted with that hoor.

Kelly No? Why have you come?

Gill laughs. Kelly looks confused. Gill looks at her. Kelly says nothing.

Gill Alright. You lead the way, missus. I suppose we'll get there when you're good and ready.

Kelly Okay . . .

Gill looks at the wall with the 'Give HIM Thanks' graphic.

Gill Tell me about all this then. (*Beat.*) It's a grift, right?

Kelly No –

Gill I'm not judging, had plenty of free dinners in my time.

Kelly It's not a grift. Gill, this is me. This is who I am.

Gill Who you are? Looks a bit . . .

Kelly What?

Gill Looks a bit . . . fucking . . .

Affecting a bad American accent, a real shocker.

Howdy doody children, y'all ready for Jesus!

Kelly Our mission –

Gill Come on out, Jesus! Where ye hiding, big lad?

Kelly Our mission started in America.

Gill Your mission? To save the sinners of Ulster?

Kelly To save everyone.

Gill picks up Deadsheep.

Gill (*to Deadsheep*) What do you think of that? –

Kelly Careful with her, Gill, careful –

Gill (*loud*) Sounds very American doesn't it? Saving everyone, whether they like it or not.

Kelly looks at the door.

Fucksake wee girl.

Kelly What?

Gill Pulling a face.

Kelly I'm not –

Gill Aye you are. I'm saying to you that I like it.

Kelly I don't know how I didn't hear that.

Gill (*admonishing*) Tone. (*Beat.*) I'm saying that it's good. That it's modern. Very hip, very cool. You expect with your God stuff more . . .

Gill wags her finger.

Y'know? But this softly-softly way of doing things . . . it can be alright is what I'm saying. If you're careful with it.

Kelly Oh that's what you're saying.

Gill abruptly stops having fun. She turns on Kelly. Kelly is very conscious that Gill is still holding Deadsheep.

Gill I said watch your tone. Gives you away so it does. 'There goes a poor wee soul who's come through care.' (*Beat.*) You didn't invent being a Christian. Your Americans, they didn't invent being Christian –

Kelly I know –

Gill We was always Christians here. Always.

Kelly I know.

Gill Do you?

Kelly I do, I'm sorry.

Gill Good. (*To Deadsheep.*) What do think? Me simply appreciating the literature, and her being all 'here we go'. (*Sheep voice.*) Shocking behaviour. Unchristian behaviour. Let me have her fucking lips.

Gill play attacks Kelly with the toy.

Kelly No –

Gill Nom nom nom –

Kelly Careful –

Gill Nom nom nom –

Kelly Careful Gill. Gentle hands. She's oul now. She's been through a lot.

Gill drops the toy. Kelly picks it up quickly. She gives it a cuddle. Gill looks on with jealousy.

She needs care. She needs love.

Kelly puts Deadsheep down again, but this time somewhere further back. Gill switches attention back to the wall graphic. She whistles.

Gill You got to hand it to them. The Americans . . . they just know how to do 'God', don't they?

Kelly gets a text. She responds while Gill is talking.

That's what I always thought. When you see them. Bigger than we are. I mean not physically, of their persons. Not always. The fat ones, aye. But I'm meaning big as in the way they carry themselves. Like they know they can make you eat shit. Daddy had that about him. And they all have fucking miles of space so they do. Back garden with a canyon in it, bigger than this whole country. If you're going to have space like that . . . it's easy to get all spread out. Lose hold of the centre of yourself. If there isn't, you know . . .

Kelly (*distracted*) God.

Gill Aye, God, aye. Or something of that ilk. Something to put in the middle of you.

Kelly finishes texting.

Kelly You don't put God anywhere. He puts you where you need to be.

Gill Potato, potahto (*Beat.*) Fuck me. It's wild to be near the sea again so it is. I'd always imagined we'd end up somewhere near water.

Gill looks intensely at Kelly.

Me and you. Just us.

Kelly Well, here we are.

Gill What? Nah, not here. Christ, please not here. I'm talking water that warms you. That can sit still and not be nipping at you. Like that one. Coul. And Nipping. Nipping nipping nipping.

Kelly is uncomfortable, she looks away.

The sound. Can't get used to having it all over me like this.

Kelly's phone receives another text. As she is speaking she looks at the phone quickly but does not respond.

Kelly I can't hear anything, sure the glass on them windows is like a fist thick.

Gill I likes it better quiet. Like where I am. My own room, a lock on on it. Sharing, but never see any of them. All different hours. Different faces. And where I'm working as well, huge office park, miles away from anywhere. Cleaning work. Oh Kelly I'm loving it. Not a fucker speaks to you. Come in after everyone goes, push that big hoover up and down, up and down . . . clear the bins, bleach the toilets, no one interfering, no nipping. (*Beat.*) I'm pulling a sickie to be here. Agency doesn't like that. But I don't care. I'm here. For you. (*Beat.*) Here I am.

Gill waits expectantly.

I really don't care you know. Never been a job I couldn't chuck if the moment came . . . If it was our time –

Kelly Our time?

Gill Aye. Like we planned.

Kelly What plan?

Another text message. Kelly notices it but does not look.

Gill We always planned.

Kelly We never speak.

Gill No, before, before . . .

Kelly Before?

Gill When you were first in that place. And you were scared, I always said if you asked, if you said the word, I'd come. And we'd go. Just us.

Kelly Okay.

Gill So . . .

Kelly So . . .

Gill Fucksake.

Kelly What?

Gill Whatever game this is you're playing, this hot-cold game –

Kelly I'm not playing any game.

Gill Are they listening in? Is that it?

Gill walks around the room searching.

Hello? Hello –

Kelly Gill, no one is listening –

Gill What's changed? Did you lose your nerve? –

Kelly Gill –

Gill Is it these people?

Kelly These people are my friends.

Gill And what am I, chopped liver?

Kelly No, Gill –

Gill I'm your biggest friend. I'm the friend who dropped everything, who reared you, who –

Kelly Reared me! (*Catching herself.*) Sorry –

Gill enjoys that she has pushed a button.

Gill There's that attitude again. Aye. Missus. Reared you. Them first years, right up until the socials got their claws into you. When you were born where was Mummy but out hooring, half the time for herself, us not seeing a penny of it. Which Daddy tolerated, so he can't have been that bad can he? (*Beat.*) I was fifteen –

Kelly I know –

Gill And there was you glued to me. And all you did was sleep, eat, shite that soupy green shite. Always close. Sure, anyone that saw us, they thought I was your mummy.

Kelly checks the door.

Just talk to me, Kelly. Because I look at you now . . . I can't . . . you don't look like you're supposed to look.

Kelly How am I supposed to look?

Gill Like that wean.

Kelly I'm not.

Gill I know, I mean that wean but grown.

Kelly Maybe I've just grown another way.

Gill That's a shame, because that wean, that wean as soon as she could sit up straight I made sure could handle herself.

Gill looks at Kelly. Searching for something. She abandons the search.

Kelly Do you want to try getting dressed now?

Gill Got in some mad hour. Wild time getting here from the airport.

Kelly goes to check the messages on her phone.

Kelly Should have called me, I'm driving.

Gill I did call you.

Kelly is reading.

Kelly (*not really listening*) Oh? I must have missed you.

Gill Arrived in, couldn't remember what house number you were. And then I had this feeling it must be number three. That was always your favourite number. So it sticks in my head that way. Three still your favourite?

Kelly puts the phone down again.

Kelly I don't know. I'd have to think about it.

Gill Think about it now.

Kelly thinks.

Well?

Kelly Don't rush me. (*Beat.*) Aye, go on then, I'll stick with three.

Gill Good. Glad to hear it. Fine number the number three. Mysterious. Important. Three of a kind, that's a powerful hand.

Kelly Oh most definitely.

Gill Me, I notice a lot of things happen in threes.

Kelly squints at Gill.

Don't look at me like that. I'm saying there's me at thirty-THREE, just arriving in the town where I left you THREE YEARS AGO after Daddy kicked it on his THIRD HEART ATTACK and then . . . then I come to a door. And this door, it gives me a tingle. Because I know this door. (*Beat, then sudden and loud.*) Sixty-six!

Kelly Goodness sake woman.

Gill Double threes. Knew it was a three. Not a pure three, not in the mathematical sense.

Kelly (*agreeing*) Awk no.

Beat.

Gill And what do you think I found out at number sixty-six?

Pause. Kelly realises.

Kelly Oh no, oh Gill –

Gill So there I am, not even five in the morning –

Kelly Gill, honestly, I'm so sorry –

Gill and I'm at that door, hammering with that wee dainty knocker, dahdahdahdah, dahdahdahdah –

Kelly Oh my days.

Gill Can feel the eyes of the entire cul-de-sac on me, like dirty fingernails pushing into the skin on my back. But I'm hammering. And the door opens. And sure there's the woman herself, (*Pronouncing as 'Keeva'.*) Caoimhe –

Kelly (*pronouncing as 'Kweeva'*) Caoimhe –

Gill wobbling in front of me on that wrong-ways foot of hers –

Kelly be kind now –

Gill And I says to her straight away, can you bring me my sister? I am in need of a private word.

And (*Pronouncing as Keeva.*) Caoimhe –

Kelly KWEE-va –

Gill continues to pronounce the name as Keeva.

Gill Caoimhe, that sharp snout on her pulled right back it is, she says to me no I cannot –

Kelly I really meant to tell you –

Gill And I says to her, are you denying me a private word? Which is mine by right?
And then she says to me . . .
Awk sure, what am I doing going on and on, you'll know what she said to me.

Kelly Gill, I am an adult and I can make decisions about my own life –

Gill She says you cleared out two years ago. Only just sixteen. Sauntered out, no warning, bold as brass –

Kelly Now, houl on –

Gill Cheery-bye, dearest foster Mummy. Here ends your years of thankless service –

Kelly I did not say that –

Gill Treasure always this TK Maxx twenty-pound gift card.

Kelly It was a nice candle and a bath bomb from Lush.

Gill And I says Caoimhe –

Kelly (*quickly, quietly*) Kwee-va –

Gill how can that be? How can a numptyfuck sixteen-year-old like you –

Kelly – I'm eighteen now –

Gill How can a numptyfuck eighteen-year-old who was then only a numptyfuck sixteen-year-old be making that kind of decision? Because you forget, Kelly, I was a numptyfuck sixteen-year-old once, and I certainly never could have walked out and Daddy not dragged me back by my two nostrils and panelled the raw shite out of me.

Kelly No, of course, I should have been just like you, waited until I was thirty to leave home.

Rage pulses through Gill. She pushes it back down. When she says Caoimhe next she says it slowly and deliberately with the Kweeva pronunciation, and continues to pronounce it as Kweeva whenever the name is said.

Gill But Caoimhe, she says, Gill, you never had Harvest. (*Beat.*) What's a Harvest says I? (*Beat.*) It's a cult.

Kelly It's not a cult –

Gill Holed up at the beach –

Kelly It's not a cult –

Gill two years living in some fucking free-love fucking nutter commune –

Kelly We're Christians.

Gill laughs.

We run a housing charity.

Gill Oh aye. Fucking Waco. Fucking Bally-fucking-Jonestown this is.

Kelly We're the only ones about here doing anything for the unhoused.

Gill (*laughs*) Unhoused!

Kelly And I was already serving at the food bank, and the recovery clinic, and the re-housing programme –

Gill picks Deadsheep up.

Gill, leave her. (*Beat.*) Look, I'm saying it made sense, to me, and the church leadership thought the same –

Gill – ah yes, Pastor Friendly, so agreeable, lots of room in his beachfront compound for nubile young ladies –

Kelly – It made sense that given my age, my context, I could apply to finish up my care with them in one of the self-contained units.

Gill You're a self-contained unit.

Kelly And my case worker agreed.

Gill Madness. (*To Deadsheep.*) You okay with this? Youse two living here, working here . . .

Gill manipulates Deadsheep so the toy is shaking its head and boo-hoo-hooing.

That's okay. Get it all out.

Gill puts Deadsheep down with care.

Poor wee fella.

Kelly She's a girl.

Gill Do you know what I think? I think maybe you're not allowed to leave this place.

Kelly That's ridiculous.

Gill Is it?

Kelly I'm allowed to leave. Of course I'm allowed to leave. I might be leaving to do a teaching course in Stranmillis.

Gill You're going to be a teacher?

Kelly Early years. Unconditional offer.

Gill adjusts to this idea.

Gill That's good. That's better. When does this happen?

Kelly Next month. But I'm not sure.

Gill Why?

Kelly I . . . you won't understand. But in my heart . . . I think my vocation is here. I think . . . I know God is calling me to something greater.

Gill Oh Kelly, you've got to stop saying this shite to me.

Kelly (*frustration*) The council funds some of our projects, the housing executive . . . This is not some . . . militia . . . camped out in the hills, like, getting ready for the rapture. We heal people. That's what we do here. We are a kinship.

Gill They're not your kin –

Kelly Kinship –

Gill I'm your kin. The only kin you have left.

Kelly What we do here . . . What I do here . . . It's good.

Gill That's not what Caoimhe said.

Kelly What's Caoimhe been saying?

Gill She not earned a ticket on board the kinship? (*Beat.*) She says to me they were at your school –

Kelly We're invited by teachers.

Gill Says to me you were coming home all excited. Caoimhe, Caoimhe, we've got to go, can we go? And her thinking, awk sure, sounds lovely. Couldn't do any harm to jam a bit of God up you.

    Kelly laughs.

But then it wasn't right.

Kelly How was it not right?

Gill That when it started up in the big space through there, a man on stage talking like a hypnotist, probably this Richard you fancy so much, lights down low, loud music, people all around crying –

Kelly Our worship, it can seem overwhelming –

Gill Scary crying. Out of breath, howling, weeping –

Kelly No –

Gill and falling down and screaming for help –

Kelly No –

Gill speaking funny.

Kelly Tongues.

Gill Speaking madey-uppy words –

Kelly It's called tongues.

Gill Tongues? Sounds a bit unhygienic if you ask me . . .

Kelly It's a gift of the Holy Spirit.

Gill A what?

Kelly An expression of devout faith –

Gill And then they see Caoimhe hirplin' in with her bent foot, and they all run at her like a pack of starved dogs –

Kelly That's not how it happened –

Gill saying they could heal her, asking if she believed God wanted her to suffer –

Kelly That isn't how it happened. We have a process. It would have been more careful. Healing is the centre of our ministry.

Gill Healing?

Kelly Recognising the power of the spirit to heal.

  Beat.

Gill Faith healing?

Kelly You see . . .

Gill laughs.

I knew if I said . . . I knew you'd call it that. Which makes it sound cheap. When it's anything but. Because it's the most precious gift –

Gill Holy Christ.

Kelly What?

Gill You really are one of them.

Kelly I've seen it, Gill. I've been part of it.

Gill Oh fuck me, fuck me, fuck me . . . –

Kelly There was a woman. She came to us with cancer –

Gill . . . fuck me!

Kelly It's true. Cancer. All through her. The doctors, they'd given up.

Gill And what did youse do? Lick it out of her with them gifted tongues?

Kelly Stop.

Gill I'd like to meet this woman, hear her side of it.

Kelly You already have.

Gill Oh aye?

Kelly You cut her head open. (*Beat.*) I've seen people transformed.

Gill All I know is Caoimhe said she was mortified. Begged you not to come back.

Kelly We talked about it, but I decided –

Gill Says they made you freeze her out.

Kelly That's not true.

Gill So you have been keeping in touch?

Kelly No . . . Look, when you're a Christian –

Gill I'm a Christian, Caoimhe's a Christian –

Kelly I know –

Gill Houl on . . . (*Mischievous.*) Papes . . . do them lot definitely count as Christian?

Kelly When you're anyone and you believe in something . . . like this . . . That's about changing the world, about being that change in the world . . . you have to constantly think about and evaluate your relationships.

Gill Is that so?

Kelly Because sometimes people don't want you to grow like you need to . . . or it's not that they are against you . . . it's just that you can't be yoked is how we put it –

Gill Yoked?

Kelly Aye, like if you had a pair of oxen and they pulled in different directions –

Gill Why would I have a pair of oxen?

Kelly I mean people.

Gill Then say people then. Say what you mean –

Kelly People pulling in different directions can be dangerous.

Gill For who?

Kelly For both of us.

Gill is walloped by this remark.

(*Hastily correcting herself.*) Both of them. What I mean is –

Gill So I came. Here. To the beach. Because that's where she said youse had built your temple. There above the dunes, on the oul golf greens. But it didn't look how I expected.

Kelly is nodding.

There was a lot of families.

Kelly Yes, see –

Gill And a bouncy castle.

Kelly Two bouncy castles. And face painting. We do all the new baptisms together, on one day right at the end of summer, make a day of it for everyone.

Gill And then this girl came up to me, dressed like you. Comes right to me. And she points up at this place and asks me if I'm coming home.

Kelly We call it that, home.

Kelly displays the message on her T-shirt.

Gill Home for daft wee girls.

Kelly Home for anyone. If they want to be here.

Gill Aye, no thanks. You can keep your cult.

Kelly We're not a cult –

Gill Fuck me, nearly skipped the best part.

Gill goes to her jacket and pulls out a bar of soap.

Handed me this so she did. Your wee twin. Handing it to me like it was a present. Says I should get myself clean.

Gill laughs.

Cheeky besom.

Kelly She wasn't . . . It's not the way she was taught to speak to people.

Gill You need to be taught that?

Kelly To do it right. There's a process.

   Gill laughs.

If you want to hear what people are really trying to tell you.

Gill I'm guessing most of the time it's 'Get the fuck away from me'.

Kelly Fine.

Gill Awk don't take it thick. Teach me then.

Kelly Teach you?

Gill The process.

Kelly No . . . I can't just . . . There's like seven modules.

   Gill laughs.

I've only just completed it –

Gill Houl on. Please, please tell me you have a certificate in talking shite.

Kelly It's a process we're all encouraged to learn –

Gill Have you had it framed? –

Kelly Whatever our role here, we learn a verified therapeutic process, a straightforward process that allows people to open up. That's all she was doing, trying to hear you. To help you.

   Gill looks at the soap.

She was trying something . . . theatrical. To get your attention. A conversation starter. More like . . . she's meaning Jesus is the soap.

   Gill lets the soap slip out of her hand.

Gill Oops! Sorry, Jesus. Fuck me he's a slippery wee fella –

32

Kelly Gill –

Gill Awk he's alright. Sure he's had worse.

Kelly You know full well what she was meaning.

Gill She's lucky she didn't get a thump. Calling me unclean.

Kelly She didn't mean you were dirty. What did she look like?

Gill Tan. Slug eyebrows. Gurn on her like she'd huffed a bag of glue.

Kelly Bronagh.

Gill Saying to me unclean.

Kelly Bronagh.

Gill Saying to me like she could see it on me, something that pure disgusted her –

Kelly I'll speak to her. She's new.

Gill That's what your Caoimhe woman was telling me about this place. Tell you too if you'd listen. All the fucking Bronaghs. Thinking they have a right. Saying they'll pray for you. Putting their hands on you. Saying you're unclean. That's a control. That'll be all your Richard's design –

Kelly No –

Gill A way of softening you up. Making you behave –

Kelly Richard isn't making anyone do anything.

Gill Wouldn't have to. You'll all be doing it for him.

Kelly Doing what?

Gill Watching each other.

Kelly snorts.

Oh no? That's not what this is? Kelly, I know how this works.

Kelly This is the same as when you'd visit me in the children's home, or at Caoimhe's. Always telling me keep down, keep quiet. Well I didn't do that Gill, and look what I found . . . A world of love.

Gill Oh I don't doubt that. They must all love you. I'm sure you give them lots to therapise . . . (*Beat.*) Do they know your mummy was a hoor? (*Beat.*) Do they?

Kelly You think you're being shocking. But you're not.

Gill Am I not?

Kelly No. We don't use that kind of language here. It's dehumanising. The projects we've done with sex workers, they're projects that reframe –

Gill Projects you've done with dirty hoors. (*Beat.*) Do they know what she did to you?

Kelly bites her tongue.

What?

Kelly Have you ever tried to imagine what it was like for Mummy?

Gill Imagine? I don't have to imagine, Kelly, I was there.

Kelly So was I.

Gill Of course, how could I forget . . . You were that one in the corner, drawing faces on your fingers and giving them all wee kisses. Tell me all about it then. Tell me what you remember.

Kelly I remember her smile.

Gill Aww. Her smile. Do you know I think I'm seeing it now too . . . this ghost you've . . . you've conjured so you have. But it's so hard to tell, isn't it? Under all them layers of hoor emulsion. Is that her actual smile, or just the one she's painted on? (*Beat.*) What stays with me, Kelly, is the living nightmare of her abducting her seven-year-old daughter in some strung-out frenzy –

Kelly She did not abduct me –

Gill Yes she fucking did –

Kelly It wasn't an abduction, not technically –

Gill She took you and she left you alone and starving with a bunch of junkies for three days –

Kelly Houl on.

Gill before disappearing off the face of the earth –

Kelly Houl on. (*Beat.*) It was one day.

Gill laughs.

It's on record. It was one day and one night and one morning and then the police had me. And she didn't . . .

Gill She didn't what?

Kelly I don't think she meant to leave me.

Gill Based on fucking what?

Kelly He . . .

Gill He?

Kelly Daddy created a situation . . .

Gill snorts.

and she was offered an opportunity, and maybe that opportunity had conditions –

Gill Situations, conditions, conditional situations . . . you auditioning for the news? Sure he was something our daddy. I'll not deny that. But her . . . she could be sitting, playing with your hair, saying – (*Mimes stroking a child's hair.*) how pretty, how lovely, just a pet aren't you, a pretty thing, you're my pretty pet, and then like that – (*Closes her*

35

fist and yanks the air.) And it wasn't about the damage in the moment. It was the knowing that the trap had been set long ago. And that everything that had felt . . . it was just bait. (*Beat.*) Do you therapise about me?

Kelly No.

Gill Do you?

Kelly No, Gill.

Gill Bet you don't remember any smiles from me. Just do this, go here –

Kelly Of course I do.

Gill How did you explain me to Pastor Friendly? To get me allowed up here.

Kelly Everyone is allowed here –

Gill What did you say to him about me?

   Pause.

Kelly I told him I'd met you recently.

Gill Oh my word Kels, have you been feeding porky pies to Big Daddy Richard?

Kelly I told him I'd met you during Street Reach, which is when we find people, on the street, and we ask them to let God in.

Gill Has he lost his keys?

Kelly I said you'd come back and found me again today, because you were in crisis . . . And he agreed. God was asking me to go with you and heal you.

Gill Get the fuck away from me with that. Is that what this is? Is that why I'm here? So you can heal me?

Kelly Maybe . . . I don't know . . . I have no idea why you're here –

Gill shakes her head.

Gill You do, stop saying that you don't when you do, you do, you know fine rightly, because it was you –

Kelly But I know the way you were acting, it wasn't right. Coming at us like that.

Gill I wasn't –

Kelly The noise you were making in the water, scaring people, hitting at people –

Gill Stop –

Kelly Gill I think you're hurting.

Gill (*angry*) I said stop that. (*Beat.*) I saw you there and I was worried.

Kelly Worried? About what?

Gill I'd come for you and you weren't where you were supposed to be –

Kelly I meant to tell you –

Gill You made me look for you –

Kelly I made you? Houl on –

Gill And I found you. I found you, I saw you in the distance, in the water, but something was missing –

Kelly Nothing is missing.

Gill Why are you pretending?

Kelly I'm not.

Gill You are pretending to me, I know it, I know you, and I saw you, I saw you were in trouble –

Kelly In the water?

Gill No –

Kelly I was fine, I was doing something beautiful, something I would love to tell you more about –

Gill No.

Gill focuses herself.

She's putting the soap in my hand –

Kelly Bronagh, aye –

Gill and she's nattering and nattering at me . . . all this double-Dutch nonsense like you're speaking now . . . and then . . . it's like something reached down and turned the volume all the way up on every sound around us. I'm hearing every sound in the world at once . . . and I look down and I'm not there.

Kelly You've disappeared?

Gill No, I mean, in my head, I'm so fucking wired already . . . and in my head, sometimes I go places if I'm not concentrating like I should –

Kelly You hallucinate?

Gill No. I just . . . I can't concentrate.

Kelly I don't know what you mean –

Gill I can't concentrate! I can't concentrate! How else do you want me to fucking say it? I'm looking at this soap, and all this noise, and I'm not concentrating the way I should, and then I'm not on the beach anymore.

Kelly You've left, you've walked away –

Gill No, that's not it. You're not getting me –

Kelly Gill –

Gill I'm back there. Home. She was talking about home. The wee girl. And I thought, our house. So I'm back there. I'm fifteen again. But I'm not, I'm my age now, but you, you're just born, and the health visitor is packing up her

38

scales, and saying to me that you're thin, you're not the weight you need to be, and why hadn't I been feeding you?

And I'm thinking so what? This wean's not my problem. Go get Mummy out of bed, out of her fucking pity party, fucking read her the riot act. And then I look at you. And Christ, Kelly, this fear, it fills me until I'm nothing but fear, because I see you there on the floor, all bones, squalling, these black eyes on me, and I know, it's clear like nothing else. She's right. It's me. It's me or it's no one.

But then the ground gives way underneath me, and I'm back on these dunes, and time is missing, and my legs are moving, I'm running, and I'm falling down now, tumbling in the sand. And I get up and I can see all of these people gathered at the water, watching something. And I look and I see. These shapes out past the crowds, past where the tide breaks, these shapes out there in the water, stretching, like the last stitches, holding the sky to the sea, before everything comes apart. The noise of that in my head.

Kelly's phone buzzes. She looks at it, but doesn't go to it.

And the littlest of those little stitches breaks loose, a woman. A girl. You. I know it, instantly, that's you, that's Kelly. I've found you. I've done it. I've come back to you. The truth of it was bursting through me. But I can't think on it too long because the other shapes, they're twisting around you, and from where I am, I can't see you anymore, not clearly, I'm seeing . . . I'm seeing only the trueness of you, of you, of this, of the moving of body and water, the last strength of you bleeding out into the sky, the strength that I gave you, my strength, all of me that I put in you to keep you alive when no one else wanted you alive.

And I've flown down the beach, I'm in the shallow and the wet sand, and on my knees, and then, changed now, in the wind, I hear everyone around me shouting. And the noise, the noise, and I look for you in it, but where are you? I'm fucking losing it, you're gone, and it's these creatures pawing at me, pulling me . . . And I . . . I . . .

And, well, you're not fucking gone are you. You're right there (*Laughs.*) sat with me in the surf. Telling me calm down you mad cow. Kelly, I am sorry I hurt that woman, I am . . . but all of you . . . putting hands over me, pulling at me, Jesus Christ Gill, I can't . . . I can't have that . . .

Gill goes to her jacket and pulls out a vape pen. She tries to use it, but it's water damaged. She chucks it back at her jacket.

Kelly Does this happen to you a lot? Losing time?

Gill It's easier when people keep their distance.

There's a knock at the door.

When there's quiet.

Gill is looking out the window.

The noise of them waves. Is it just me or is it getting louder?

Kelly checks her phone.

Kelly Frig.

Another knock.

Gill Who's that?

Kelly Houl on . . . just let me . . .

Kelly texts. She looks at the door.

(*Distracted.*) They know we want to do this the right way.

Gill Do what?

There is a knock at the door again. Kelly puts down her phone.

Kelly Sake. Sorry Gill, one moment.

Kelly moves towards the exit and meets Sarah coming the other way. Sarah is wearing a 'Welcome Home' T-shirt, just like Kelly's. She has a big plaster on her forehead.

*The phone rings. Gill's attention fixes on the phone,
she has her back to Kelly and Sarah. The room starts to
lose its edges.*

(*To Sarah.*) Not now.

Sarah looks past Kelly to Gill.

(*Firm.*) Not now.

*During this interaction Gill approaches the phone. As she
gets nearer, the sound of the ringing distorts. Gill sees
that her action can affect the environment. Sarah departs
and Kelly returns. The room becomes solid.*

Leave that, let it ring out.

Gill You called me. Last night.

Kelly Umm, no I didn't.

Gill Stop this Kelly, please, I need us to talk plainly.

Kelly Are you sure it was me calling?

Gill No one else has my number.

Kelly (*incredulous*) No one else has your number?

Gill No. Just you.

*Gill speaks again before Kelly can figure out how to
respond to this.*

And the agency. For work, you know. For the rota. (*Beat.*)
That's where I was. I was at work. Last night. Just starting.
The second-floor toilets. I had the phone sitting on the
cistern in front of me. Always keep it in sight, just in case,
and then it comes alive, and the sound of it clattering about
on the loo, my heart . . .

Gill pounds her chest.

Because I knew . . . I was at work, it wasn't going to be
work calling . . . so it must be you, reaching out to me . . .

(*Struggling.*) and I answered, and a voice said come home, and then nothing –

Kelly I said come home?

Gill Aye –

Kelly That was it? Nothing else? –

Gill No. First you sneezed this big dirty sneeze.

Kelly laughs.

This isn't a joke.

Kelly I'm sorry Gill, I'm not meaning –

Gill Silence, then a sneeze, then Come Home. And then you hung up.

Kelly Why didn't you call me back?

Gill I did. Again and again and again –

Kelly Is it possible that you were dreaming –

Gill – Do not say that to me –

Kelly – like at the baptism Gill, losing time –

Gill Do not fucking say that to me. I'm not touched. I know what is and what isn't. Maybe not always every moment. But I know.

Kelly How?

Gill Because it started with you speaking to me.

Kelly I thought it started with me howling out my nose.

Gill Stop fucking around.

Kelly I'm not.

Gill When it happens . . . When I'm gone, sometimes it's good, it starts off nice, I can see whole other worlds, Kelly.

I can go places. Better places. Places I've never been but that I know side to side, top to bottom. And nearly always I find you. In the centre of everything. And you look good, like how you're supposed to look, better than this . . .

Kelly Thanks.

Gill No . . . I mean, you're dressed like you dressed up for me. And it makes me feel . . . Fuck, I don't know . . . Special. I feel special to you. But if I try to speak to you, if I even say one word, you turn from me and this other world comes –

Kelly Other world –

Gill A world where I shouldn't be. Where it's not nice.

Kelly Gill –

Gill That's how I know the difference. Because this time it was you. You weren't turning from me. You were coming to me and speaking to me and what you were saying was Come Home.

Gill goes to her bag.

Here, look.

Gill hands Kelly her phone.

Look at the calls. You'll see.

Kelly tries to switch the phone on.

Kelly It's not turning on.

Gill Give it.

Kelly gives the phone back.

Kelly Maybe the water.

Gill Give me yours. We'll see on yours.

Kelly pulls the phone to her chest.

43

Kelly No.

Gill Give it.

Kelly No.

Gill Hand it over.

Gill picks up Deadsheep.

Kelly You wouldn't.

Gill picks a vulnerable seam in the toy and begins to gently pull it's limbs.

You wouldn't. Gill I swear, honestly, I would never speak to you again if you harmed her even one bit.

Gill pulls slightly harder.

I swear Gill, I swear.

Gill pulls slightly harder.

No, please, here.

Kelly holds out the phone. Gill keeps pulling at Deadsheep's limbs.

Please, Gill, come on . . .

Gill tucks Deadsheep under her armpit.

Give her back.

Gill Passcode.

Kelly Give her back.

Kelly grabs for Deadsheep. Gill keeps out of Kelly's reach.

Gill I'll try your birthday . . .

Wrong passcode, Kelly grabs for Deadsheep again.

My birthday . . .

Wrong passcode. Gill looks up at Kelly. She thinks. She tries again. She is successful. Kelly stops.

Her birthday? How do you even know that?

Gill scrolls.

Lot of messages on here from Richard.

Kelly You want me to go get my diary for you to read?

Gill You weren't lying, he is very friendly.

Kelly Don't be doing that.

Gill Doing what?

Kelly Making something beautiful into something mucky.

Beat.

Gill If I was you I'd be worried by this kind of friendly.

Gill turns her attention back to the phone. She is scrolling and scrolling but not finding what she wants.

Where are my calls? (*Beat.*) Did you delete them?

Kelly No.

Gill You're lying to me.

The phone buzzes in Gill's hand. Gill looks at the message.

Kelly Is that him?

Gill holds the phone up to Kelly.

Gill 'You shouldn't do this alone.' Two kisses.

Kelly looks at the message.

Do what alone? What are you doing?

Kelly Being with you. He wanted to be here. To support me.

Gill Likes to keep you close.

Kelly Or someone, anyone, to assist, two-to-one, it's procedure –

Gill Assist you with what?

Kelly In case you might be dangerous.

Gill Like Caoimhe was dangerous?

Kelly Like people who stab people are dangerous.

Gill chucks Deadsheep at Kelly and turns her attention back to the phone. Kelly quickly picks the toy up and checks it's okay. She sighs in relief.

I told you Gill, she needs care. She needs gentle hands, gentle –

Gill (*exploding in anger*) It's a fucking toy. Christ. Thought you were supposed to be an adult . . . Stoating about with a fucking rancid oul teddy . . .

Gill holds the phone out.

Get me to your answering machine. I left you messages.

Kelly It's the only thing from Mummy that I had with me.

Gill looks at Kelly holding Deadsheep.

Gill What? The sheep? Nah, you . . . you lifted it from that first children's home. I remember. Your sticky fingers phase –

Kelly She had it with her when she came into school.

Gill Never a day in her life did she pick you up from school.

Kelly She did that one day.

Pause. Gill nods to Deadsheep.

Gill So you're saying that thing was the bait.

Kelly No –

Gill Flashing you a wee present so you'd follow –

46

Kelly No.

Gill You don't remember –

Kelly I do. Gill. I do remember. Because it was me this happened to. Not you. Me. I remember being at school, and I remember we were about to go on the computer, and I was looking forward to that because I loved getting a go on the computer, but then Mummy was there, there in the actual classroom, talking to Mrs Doone, holding Deadsheep to her like she was her baby.

And we left, we got in a car, not our car, and I remember she drove . . . she drove us for a long time, a really long time. I saw all over the back seat, all my clothes, and all these bags of crisps, shop sandwiches . . . And then we arrived, and we were in a place I'd never been before. And there was a man who hugged her and kissed her head and her hands.

And she went off into another room and he asked me, the man, he was so kind to me, he asked me if I was hungry and he poured me a bowl of Weetos and then he put on the TV and he left and went into that other room.

And then I watched TV for hours and hours and fell asleep and when I woke it was dark and there was a different man there, not the same one as before, and a woman I think, or maybe just a smaller man, and they were watching TV. And I asked them where my mummy was and they, they just, well they didn't hear me, or they, I suppose they couldn't and I looked in the room where Mummy had gone and it was empty.

But there was a mattress in there and a sleeping bag, so I got in the bed and ate some crisps, and I cuddled up with Deadsheep, all in that bag, and I slept again and when I woke that was when the police were there and there was a woman police officer and she knew my name – (*Beat.*) Mummy had told them.

Beat.

Gill No.

Kelly Yes Gill.

Gill She didn't do that.

Kelly She did. She rang in and told them where I was. Did you never wonder how they found me so quickly?
    It wasn't bait, Gill.

Kelly squeezes Deadsheep close.

It was love. It was always love.

Gill How do you know?

Kelly Because you know love when you feel it.

Gill No. I mean, how do you know it was her . . . her that told the police . . . it might have been something else that led them to you –

Kelly When I was arranging moving out of Caoimhe's, a man in child services, the man with the forms, he said I could have a copy of my case file if I wanted. And I read it and it was there. 'Child's mother called in and said she was sorry and gave child's location and hung up the call. Attempts to call her back unsuccessful.' (*Beat.*) I have it here, in my room, I can get it, if you want to take a look –

Gill Daddy tried to get you back. (*Beat.*) But by then it was all happening, and they wouldn't . . . He had all them convictions. But he always said, just you wait Gilly, she'll come back to us. She'll get a few years on her, soon they won't know where she is half the time. And that's when we'll get her. Back where she belongs.

Pause.

Kelly I know you wouldn't have let that happen.

Gill shakes her head.

You wouldn't have.

Gill You should have been with family.

Kelly That wasn't a family, Gill. It was a monster that was eating us all alive. And Mummy knew that. She was saving me.

Gill (*barely more than reflex*) Saving herself.

Kelly No. She knew, she knew what she was dealing with inside her after all them years, she knew she was in no fit state to be anybody's mummy.

Gill You're getting an awful lot from one phone call to the police.

Kelly's phone rings. She takes it from Gill. Gill offers no resistance. Kelly silences the call. She is thinking through her next steps.

Are you not going to get that?

Kelly I know what it's about.

Gill Won't they worry? (*Beat.*) Why would you delete all those calls? I don't understand you like this.

The phone rings again. Kelly looks at it and shakes her head. She silences the call.

Kelly I think I should step out for a minute.

Gill No you shouldn't.

Kelly moves away from Gill to the door.

When I arrived –

Kelly is about to leave.

Don't go.

Kelly Only for a minute. I need to . . . Maybe you could get dressed while I'm gone. You'll be more comfortable.

Gill I wanted to look good for you.

Kelly's phone starts ringing again.

(*Urgent.*) When I got here, I saw the water for the first time. All that noise . . . You called it God's majesty . . .

Kelly silences it again.

(*Tripping over herself.*) Whatever it is, past it, I keep trying to get past this noise, this nipping, but I can't, it gets louder if I try, but if we can get past it, me and you, if we can do it, get past where we can see, the space out there Kelly, it's forever, I read that somewhere, it doesn't stop expanding –

Kelly Gill –

Gill Imagine how far we could go –

Kelly I need to speak to Richard –

Gill Something is missing. I can't see what it is because you're being sneaky.

Kelly No.

Gill You're not letting me see it, but I know it.

Kelly No, Gill –

Kelly's phone buzzes, she looks at it.

Gill But, I'm saying, we can leave it here, let it stay missing, find us our own space, just us –

Kelly Richard –

Gill I don't care about anyone else. Just you, Kelly –

Kelly I need to speak to him, but I promise I will be right back –

Kelly is leaving.

Gill I shouldn't have left you. I should have taken you with me. When Daddy died –

Kelly You couldn't have taken me.

Gill Why not?

Kelly I wasn't yours to take.

Gill I should have spoken to you, explained –

Kelly You were scared.

Gill No, that's not it . . . that isn't it. I stopped being scared. For the first time in my life I wasn't scared. Because I knew you were safe. I had done it, I'd kept you safe. You don't know . . . what it's like . . . worrying about a wee thing, every day, a wee thing that wasn't even yours, that you didn't want . . . I don't mean that, I didn't mean that –

Kelly Gill –

Gill But he'd been saying more and more, saying it's time. Would I talk to you, since I was the one allowed to visit. He had a phone, he wanted me to give it you, as a present. And I knew, I knew, I knew what that kind of present was, for me to be asked to give a present like that, like you were one of them, like one of them girls, stupid wee girls, like you could ever be one of them, like I would ever give you a present like I gave them his presents . . . and I told him no. I told him no. I told him that again and again, that wasn't the way. He said I was confused, but I wasn't confused. I knew what that kind of present meant, and I told him, and sometimes when I told him, I was so loud and so angry. Too angry, far too angry. He'd have to hold my arms, until I calmed down. He'd say to me houl on wee girl, I can't let you out in the world like this. Imagine the damage you could do.

Kelly It's okay.

Gill I wouldn't ever be that angry with you.

Kelly I know you wouldn't –

Gill But then it didn't even matter. Because it was his own heart. It did it for us. I didn't even need to be angry. I didn't need to do anything, I just needed to let it happen. It started. And I went into another room. And when I came back out it had happened –

Kelly's phone rings again. Kelly lets it ring.

And it was over. And maybe I should have gone to you, maybe –

Kelly I understand –

Gill I just, I had to go, I had to . . . That relief –

Kelly I get it.

Gill And you looked, you seemed happy.

Kelly I was okay.

Gill But it was a mistake.

Kelly No –

Gill Because look where you've ended up.

Kelly I'm where I am supposed to be.

Gill No, I know those words. I know them.

Kelly No –

Gill Then why won't you speak to me?

Kelly I don't know if you're ready.

There is a knock at the door that sounds like a thunderclap. Gill is startled. There is another knock, even louder.

Gill (*small, frightened*) Help me.

Kelly hasn't heard the knocking. Thinking Gill is asking her for help, she smiles at her sister. The door opens.

Kelly Yes.

Gill collects herself.

Gill (*determined*) You have to come with me now.

Sarah is standing in the doorway. When she calls to Kelly we hear a pre-recorded male voice played at roughly the same time as Sarah's, also calling Kelly's name.

Sarah *and* **Male Voice** (*off*) Kelly.

Gill (*fast*) It can be just us/

Sarah *and* **Male Voice** (*off*) Kelly.

Kelly I've got to go.

Kelly tries to move away, but Gill grabs her.

Gill No.

Kelly kisses Gill's hands and Gill backs away.

No, ask, you have to ask first. Why don't you know that anymore, who are you? –

Kelly I will be right back. Get dressed.

Kelly exits. Gill moves to the door and then away. She closes her eyes. She is humming to herself. She is searching. The noise of everything grows louder.

Gill (*murmuring*) Speak to me. Come on, baby, speak –

Kelly's phone buzzes with a new message. Gill keeps humming.

Not like this . . .

Kelly's phone buzzes again. Gill opens one eye and looks at the phone. It buzzes. She closes her eyes and keeps humming.

Not like this . . .

The phone start ringing. Gill shakes her head and hums. She holds out her hand and the ringing distorts. She closes the ringing in her fist and it becomes muffled, but soon the sound forces its way out between her fingers.

53

The phone answers itself. We hear a pre-recorded dialogue between Gill and the Male Voice we just heard calling for Kelly. In the room, Gill listens to the dialogue and murmurs along to both parts. It is a script she has written for herself, pieced together from multiple memories.

To begin with no one says anything. We hear the Male Voice, he is breathing. And then he lets out a big dirty sneeze.

Phone Gill Bless you.

Male Voice Who's this? (*Beat.*) Who's this?

Phone Gill It's Gillian.

Male Voice Hello Gillian. Can I speak to your mother?

Phone Gill She isn't here.

Male Voice Oh.

Phone Gill She's gone.

Gill stops murmuring along. She begins making that low hum again. She goes to the phone.

Male Voice That's a shame. I was hoping to see a friend tonight.

Gill hangs up the phone, but it keeps speaking.

Phone Gill We . . . I have other friends.

Gill hammers the phone with her fingers trying to end the call. Her humming becomes the words 'Here I am.'

Would you like me to give you the number of a wee friend of mine you might like?

Male Voice Yes please –

Gill drops the phone.

Gill Here I am here I am here I am here I am here I am here I am here I am –

54

The room lights up. Kelly has returned, this time with Sarah. Kelly is stood near Gill, and Sarah is sat away from them. Kelly is no longer wearing the wetsuit or the branded T-shirt. She has changed into comfortable clothes. Sarah is also no longer wearing the T-shirt and is similarly dressed to Kelly.
  Gill has lost time again. She is disorientated.

Kelly You've not dressed.

Gill Oh?

Kelly I wanted you to get dressed.

Gill I can do it now –

Kelly No –

Gill If you like –

Kelly I'm sorry that took so long.

Gill It did?

  Sarah blows her nose loudly.

Kelly Yes.

Gill I didn't notice –

Kelly (*to Sarah*) Bless you.

Sarah Sorry.

Gill Who's that sitting there? Is it your assistant? (*Beat.*) The assistant they wanted for you –

Kelly Oh –

Gill To be safe from me –

Kelly Oh. No. (*Beat.*) Gill, I'm sorry I left you –

Gill You said that and I forgive you –

Kelly It wasn't my intention –

Gill let's go –

Kelly but, there were conversations that needed to happen . . .

Gill He spoke to me.

Kelly What? On the phone? Who?

Gill shakes her head.

Richard? –

Gill No, it was from before –

Kelly What did this person say to you?

Gill Nasty untrue things. (*Whispered.*) Isn't that your woman . . . the cancer granny? Do you need me to go over and apologise?

Kelly Gill, listen to me. Something wonderful has happened –

Gill Is that what I need to do to get this done with? –

Kelly No. Gill –

Gill I will.

Kelly No –

Gill I'll do anything now, anything you ask –

Kelly Then listen. I want to try and explain this to you. I did something new today.

Gill Good for you.

Kelly I helped baptise someone.

Gill I know, I was there.

Kelly I'd never done that before.

Gill Kelly, does she really need to be here?

Kelly But Richard thought I should be the one.

Gill I'm not going to hurt you –

Kelly Listen –

Gill Why would I hurt you? –

Kelly Listen, let me say this –

Gill Creeping me out she is, just sitting there –

Kelly Listen.

Gill I'm not sure who I'm listening to.

Kelly Who else would it be? I'm speaking to you aren't I?

Gill Yes . . . but . . . you're different –

Kelly And that's how you know. We're speaking. It's the real me, it's the real me and the real you.

Gill Yes. Yes. You're right. Of course –

Kelly Here, all we ask for is the real you.

Gill What's that?

Kelly We can find her. And when we do you can leave everything else behind. And so what's left, you see, it's the you that was made to be loved, in deep real colour –

Gill I love you.

Kelly nods her head.

Kelly Hm hmm hm hmm. But that feeling . . . That feeling everyone gets in the beginning, the feeling of finally finding yourself, oh it's big hook. But it can fade. You know. It degrades. You need to care for it. And that's about discipline, okay?

Gill We could go anywhere together.

Kelly Or we could stay here and go so much further.

Gill shakes her head.

I know it's hard. At one point I was ready to give up. I'd dug out your number even.

Gill And that's why I came –

Kelly No –

Gill Because you told me come home.

Kelly No, no, listen. This was ages ago. I'm saying I didn't do it, I didn't.

Gill You did.

Kelly No. I didn't. Because right at that moment there she was.

Gill looks at Sarah. Kelly pulls her back.

She came to us. Out of nowhere.

Gill Her?

Kelly She was referred to us. She'd been sleeping rough. We were asked if we had a bed for a woman in her fifties, cancer diagnosis. And I saw her . . . And I . . . but I didn't have time, because of her body . . .

Gill Her body?

Kelly Gill, it was coming apart –

Gill Oh right, yes, the cancer.

Kelly Coming apart right in front of me.

Gill (*to Sarah*) Congratulations on getting through it, missus.

Sarah Thank you –

Gill looks away.

Kelly And she's here with us, out of nowhere, and I'm thinking only of myself, of my own fear.

Gill What had you to be afraid of?

Kelly It looked like she would break.

Gill She looks fine.

Kelly She is fine. Because Richard came to me. And he said, Kelly, I know this is hard for you. But God needs you to pray for her. You specifically, Kelly. He needs you. She needs you. (*Beat.*) You really don't recognise her?

Gill squints.

Gill No . . . Who is she?

Kelly That's incredible . . . (*To Sarah.*) Isn't that incredible?

Sarah gives only a gentle nod. It is not that she wants to reject Kelly's enthusiasm outright, it is simply that experience tells her she should treat Gill with more caution.

Gill Was she one of your case workers?

Kelly Gill, the process is so clear here, Richard, he showed me what was in the way of her recovery. What was in the way . . . It was me. I was in the way. He made it so clear. How selfish I was to hold back anything anymore, from him, from God. That if I had faith, true faith, then she wouldn't hurt ever again. So I went to her, and she didn't want me there at first – (*To Sarah.*) did you? (*To Gill.*) – and we prayed for her, and . . . And I did it, I put my hand on her.

And I begged. I let all the doubt fall away. All the fear. And I begged. I was casting into the furthest place I could imagine, my hands on her, whispering into eternity.

And after, she got up, and she thanked us. She thanked me. And I couldn't . . . not immediately, that took a while. We kept our distance.

But I, honestly, I was barely human, I think I fell through the next weeks. There was no floor or ceiling to me anymore. And then, it wasn't even two months later, but she found out the good news. And she came back to me, Gill.

Gill starts to see what she doesn't want to see.

59

And she caught me. I stopped falling. She laid me down. And said it's okay, look, I'm okay, and she was just . . . where there was nothing . . . I mean look at her, Gill . . .

Gill will not look. She closes her eyes.

You can see yourself . . . where there had been nothing, now there was a gleaming gas giant, rising above me. Healed. Doctors couldn't say a thing about it. But she said she knew why. It was me. Us. It was the spirit moving through our bodies, through our voice.

And so now I've seen that, Gill. And it's not about seeing, it's not about that, it's not some show . . . but when you do get to see it. When He lets you see it. Gill, I want to show you that. Will you open your eyes?

Gill No.

Kelly I don't think it's a coincidence that you came here today.

Gill I came because you said come home.

Kelly I didn't. I didn't, Gill. God did.

Kelly turns to Sarah.

And look who else He called home.

Sarah waves from her seat.

Sarah Hello Gillian.

Gill opens her eyes and looks at Sarah.

Kelly I always told you she'd come back. (*Beat.*) And today. She took a really big step. Didn't you?

Sarah I did, yes.

Kelly Well . . . How did it feel?

Sarah looks unsure. She watches Gill.

Tell us.

Kelly laughs. Sarah laughs a little as well.

Sarah Good.

Kelly It felt good. Yes. With all of us with you to see your commitment. Even though we were a little interrupted at the end.

Kelly laughs. Sarah laughs. She is still watching Gill.

Sarah Yes.

She touches her plaster.

Boop.

Kelly Gill, I wasn't sure she should come in here, not to begin with, wasn't sure after how you reacted to first seeing her, but she's insisted . . . been insisting to me this whole time –

Gill spits at Sarah.

Gill! Mum –

Sarah It's okay.

Gill starts humming. She stares at Sarah and shakes her head. Sarah stares back.

Kelly Gill.

Gill grabs her keys from the ground.

No.

Kelly shields Sarah with her body.

No.

Gill Move.

Gill keeps humming.

Move.

Kelly Not until you calm down.

Gill Move.

Gill advances. Kelly holds an arm out.

Kelly Don't you touch her –

Sarah Kelly –

Kelly I won't let you touch her.

Gill knocks Kelly's arm away. Kelly wraps herself around Sarah.

Jesus loves you, Gill. He loves you. He loves you. He loves you. He does. He loves you.

Gill moves away. She moves to the exit. She moves back again. She sinks to her knees.

You see. Don't you? You see He's here. He's here and he loves you. He loves you. He loves you so much Gill, so so much.

Gill is shaking her head.

Mummy has something she would like to say to you.

Kelly waits to let Gill respond. Gill remains motionless.

Mummy?

Sarah (*unsure*) Now?

Kelly Yes. If you're ready.

Sarah looks at Gill on the ground. She reaches into her handbag. She pulls out a tissue and blows her nose.

I've it written down, Gillian. We thought . . . I thought that would be better. So . . .

Sarah reaches into her bag again and takes out and unfolds an A4 piece of paper. She squints at it. She sighs. She goes back to her bag.

I'm sorry.

Kelly It's okay.

Sarah I hate wearing these things.

Sarah pulls out a pair of reading glasses and puts them on. She quickly glances over the text. She seems about to read, then stops.

Gillian, stop me if this gets to be too much.

She clears her throat.

'Dear Gillian.'

Gill laughs. Sarah stops reading and looks at Kelly.

Kelly Go on.

Sarah (*haltingly*) 'Dear Gillian. I don't know where I should begin. I will begin by saying to you that I am sorry. I do not expect your forgiveness –'

Gill stands up. She moves close to Sarah. Sarah falters, but then continues. Gill stares at Sarah. Kelly nervously watches Gill.

'I do not expect your forgiveness, but I do hope that one day –'

Kelly Gill . . .

Gill keeps her eyes locked on Sarah. She places her keys on the ground.
   Sarah has lost her place. She picks it up a little further on.

Sarah 'Back when you were born I suffered from hard drug and alcohol addiction, low self-esteem, eating disorders, undiagnosed post-natal depression, the list goes on. Back then, I did not believe I could be a happy person. This is not to excuse my part in what was done to you. I know that I allowed lines to be crossed that should never have been crossed –'

Gill goes to Sarah and snatches the page out of her hand.
She walks away with it. Kelly and Sarah watch her. She
begins as if she intends to read the page. But she doesn't
read it. She can't even look down at it. It's as if she might
give herself an injury if she tried. She scrunches up the
page and drops it on the ground.

Gill Compelling stuff.

Kelly Mummy worked hard on that.

Sarah It's okay –

Gill Oh yes, I could see. Such hard work. More than one
colour of crayon as well. Very creative.

Kelly Is there anything you want to say to her in return?

Gill laughs.

Gill Plenty.

Kelly Go on then.

Gill None of it suitable for a house of God I'm afraid.

Kelly He's heard everything.

Gill Then what need is there to say it?

Kelly I think Mummy needs to hear it from you.

Sarah Kelly –

Gill Hear what?

Kelly Hear you acknowledge what you experienced together.

Gill shakes her head.

Because of him.

Gill We're not starting on with that.

Sarah Kelly, you're rushing things.

Kelly (*annoyed*) No I'm not. You weren't here before, she
admitted to me –

Gill Admitted?

Kelly The hold he had over you –

Gill I loved my daddy –

Kelly Being able to speak some of that truth, that's the first step. The kinds of things he expected of you –

Gill Stop –

Kelly Talking to girls for him, bringing them in –

Gill Stop –

Kelly like Mummy had to do before she escaped –

Gill (*through clenched teeth*) I'm not her.

Gill balls her fists. Sarah sees.

Sarah (*quick*) Gillian.

Gill freezes.

Kelly, go easy.

Gill (*to Sarah*) This is you. In my head already. Stirring.

Kelly You have both been through so much. But here. Within these walls, that's where that violence ends.

Gill You sure about that?

Sarah Breathe, Gillian.

Gill Shut your fucking trap, you oul hoor.

Kelly Who's that speaking if not Daddy?

Gill moves close to Kelly.

Gill (*whispered*) I can be more careful with my language.

Kelly No, Gill. You don't get it –

Gill It's having her near, that's what it's been, but if we go –

Kelly She's not what we need to get away from –

65

Gill Of course she is. Her, him, you're right, it's him as well, both of them, they're a package, fifty-fifty –

Kelly No, Gill, it isn't about her and him. It's about him and you. (*Beat.*) It's about getting away from the you that became him. I want to help you to do that. It's possible. Look at what I did for Mummy –

Sarah Kelly, don't –

Kelly God brought her back when He did because He knew I was strong enough –

Sarah Kelly love –

Kelly But that strength started with her. Her moment of grace. That she had the bravery that day to say no. And to take me. To save me.

Gill Then why didn't she save me? What was wrong with me. (*To Sarah.*) You was my mummy too.

Sarah Gill.

Gill Why not me?

Sarah And you would have come would you?

Gill Aye. (*Beat.*) Maybe.

Kelly Maybe! –

Sarah (*to Kelly, stern*) Whisht.

Sarah pauses to let Gill's answer hang there.

Gill (*unconvincing*) I'd need to have known, I'd needed to have made sure, something big like that.

Sarah Aye. Of course.

Gill You can't just do that, there was an order to things, an order –

Sarah It wasn't that long before, was it? I know it wasn't, because that's what first set me thinking. When that neighbour woman came round, spoke to us. Came to the door with a big box, like she was bringing over something that had been delivered to her by accident. Just in case he had anyone watching. And there, quick as anything she says at the bottom of this box I've written my number. Says I've seen you. I've seen this house. I've seen what goes on here. You call me anytime. I'll take you to the women's refuge over in Lisburn. My sister works there. I'll bring you straight to her. And then quick as she came she was away. And I remember, still, you looking at wee Kelly, hope dancing all across your face.

Gill is silent.

He took so much pleasure letting me know you'd told him all about it as soon as he got home. You'll have wanted to be quick about it, telling him, worried maybe I'd go on and get in there first. And probably I would of. Because that's how it worked in our house.

Sarah suppresses a sneeze.

Sorry. (*Continuing.*) And I know, Gillian, I know better than anyone, so hear me, listen to me would you when I say this, I know how deep he was in our two heads –

Sarah suppresses a sneeze.

(*Quickly.*) Kelly, could you grab me a tissue from my bag.

Kelly grabs her a tissue.

Thank you.

Sarah waits to sneeze.

Of course, it's gone now. And Gillian –

Sarah suddenly sneezes a big dirty sneeze.

Oh.

She blows her nose.

Sorry. Sometimes they just sneak up on you don't they?

Gill looks at Sarah. She looks at Kelly.

Gill It was God that called me last night was it?

Kelly looks at Sarah.

You need to keep a better eye on your phone, Kelly. There's a rogue element in these parts.

Kelly (*confused*) Mummy?

Gill (*to Sarah*) Trying to make out like it was only ever Daddy playing mind games.

Sarah looks directly at Gill and says nothing.

Kelly It doesn't matter, God, He does His work through us –

Gill (*sudden*) Okay, I'm up for it, let's do it.

Kelly What?

Gill Heal me. Do your process.

Sarah Gillian –

Gill I'm a fast learner.

Kelly looks between Gill and Sarah.

I mean it. Let's do it. Let's get started. I'm ready.

Kelly You're making fun.

Gill I'm not. (*Beat.*) I'm not. I want this.

Gill grabs Kelly's hand. Kelly looks nervously at Gill, and then back at Sarah.

Don't look at her. You've done her. It's my turn, look at me. How do we start?

Kelly (*unsure*) Sometimes when I can't pray I put on this white noise and it helps, and I thought, the way you've been talking about the places that you go, well I thought it could maybe –

68

Gill Aye, sure, whatever, good.

Kelly picks up her phone, she raises it to her mouth.

Kelly If it even works. (*To her phone,*) Play playlist 'focus'.

White noise plays all around them. Kelly puts the phone down, stands in front of Gill and centres herself.

So . . . Usually –

Gill Is it not a bit loud?

Kelly Oh.

Kelly picks up the phone and hands it to Gill.

Just with your finger, you set it at whatever.

Gill dials the volume back. Kelly puts down the phone and starts again.

So usually, this would start with me kind of saying what we're going to do . . . But I suppose we've kind of skipped about a bit already . . . (*Abrupt.*) What's wrong? (*Beat.*) What's wrong?

Gill Sorry, am I supposed to answer?

Kelly This has to be a dialogue.

Gill Feel like I'm at the doctor's here.

Kelly That's okay. Think of it like that. It's triage.

Gill Okay.

Kelly We're figuring things out. All three of us. Together. I'm told three is a powerful hand.

Gill laughs a little at Kelly's callback.

How long have you been feeling lonely?

Beat.

Gill I don't think I'm lonely.

Kelly Sorry, I thought you said that.

Sarah It's alright Kel, take your time now.

Kelly (*annoyed*) I am –

Gill I didn't.

Kelly No one's number but mine.

Gill And work.

Kelly That sounds lonely.

Gill There's a difference between lonely and alone.

Kelly Everybody needs people.

Gill Not everybody –

Kelly You know what, don't worry about it. Gill, can I lay my hand on you?

Facing Gill, Kelly puts her right hand on Gill's left shoulder. Gill flinches.

Mummy, you as well.

Sarah Gillian?

Gill (*to Sarah*) Just do it.

Sarah stands behind Gill. She places her hand down on Gill's right shoulder. Gill flinches.

Kelly I want to ask God right now if He'll guide us.

Pause.

Gill (*genuine*) What did he say?

Kelly opens her eyes and stops.

Kelly I can't do this if you're going to make fun –

Gill I wasn't . . . Sorry.

Gill takes Kelly's hand and puts it back on her shoulder.

Kelly Have you been hiding because of a feeling of shame?

Gill I don't feel any shame.

Kelly sighs.

I don't.

Kelly Gill. Come on.

Gill Let's leave this bit for later, we'll go back to it –

Kelly That's not how it works.

Gill I don't know how any of this is supposed to work.

Kelly It works by talking.

Gill Kelly, you've got to be careful about who's listening.

Kelly I talk to the people I love. Every day. (*Beat.*) You said before, in your head, you talk to me and I don't talk back. What do you think that means? (*Beat.*) I think that means you're scared of what I might say. (*Beat.*) What else do you think about? Apart from me.

Gill I don't know.

Kelly You don't know what you think about?

Gill I don't think about it.

Kelly Think about it.

Gill (*quiet*) Now you're the one taking the hand.

Sarah Kelly, let's leave this just now –

Kelly I'm not, Gill, I swear. God, I want you to send your spirit to us. And with it open Gill's eyes. And Gill, what I have to say to you, is that you being here, it makes me so excited.

Kelly opens her eyes.

Gill It does?

Kelly Yes. Can I kiss you?

71

Gill Yes.

Kelly kisses Gill.

Kelly Are you excited?

Gill Yes.

Kelly looks at Sarah.

Kelly (*to Sarah*) See?

Sarah smiles. Kelly closes her eyes again

And God, you told us talking is all we need to be healed.
Like your son Jesus healed the leper. Like when he said 'Be
healed'. Just those words 'Be healed'.

Gill I love you, Kelly.

Kelly We are all loved. We were all made to be loved.

Gill I love you.

Kelly opens her eyes.

Kelly Gill, what you experienced on the beach today . . .
What you experience when you go other places . . . The first
thing I thought, the very first thing, was this is prophecy.
My sister is experiencing God's word. And that's a gift only
given to the most special among us.

Gill You think I'm special?

Kelly Of course I do.

Gill smiles.

I think you're being shown the way to somewhere greater.
And you don't need to go it alone anymore.

Gill You'll come with me?

Kelly Yes.

Gill smiles.

We all will. Here, together. Richard will explain this.

Sarah takes her hand off Gill and takes a step back.

Gill Why would he be explaining anything to me?

Kelly I can only take you so far. I don't know everything.

Gill No.

Kelly But I'll still be involved.

Sarah Gillian's right, this is a family matter. And I'm sure he'll not want to stick his beak in.

Kelly No it's okay, he thinks the same.

Sarah looks at Gill.

It's okay, Gill. Richard is okay, I really cannot wait for you to meet him. Properly. He's so excited about you, just like I am.

Gill I thought he didn't know me.

Kelly Through me he has heard you.

Gill I wasn't speaking to him.

Sarah Kelly –

Kelly Gill, would you . . . Just listen to me. Listen. This is good. I was the one who was unsure, but Richard, he knew straight away, just like before, with Mummy –

Gill I wasn't speaking to him –

Kelly He told me, Kelly, when you're looking for God in everything, sometimes you miss Him standing right in front of you. He's been with us this whole time. He wants us together, all three of us, under one roof. Because that's how we'll serve Him.

Gill picks up her keys. Sarah sees this.

Sarah Gillian –

Kelly What's wrong?

Gill backs away.

Gill (*to Sarah*) I can't –

Sarah Easy now –

Gill I can't –

Sarah Calm yourself –

Kelly No, Gill, everyone can. Even someone like you.

Gill Someone like me?

Kelly I don't mean anything by it. I mean someone carrying this amount of shame.

Beat.

Gill Do you love me, Kelly?

Kelly hesitates. Gill picks up Deadsheep.

Kelly (*unimpressed*) Put her down.

Gill Tell me you love me.

Kelly Gentle hands.

Gill Why can't you tell me you love me?

Kelly does not answer.

Is honesty part of your process?

Kelly Yes.

Kelly looks at Sarah.

You know love when you feel it.

Gill What does that mean?

Kelly It isn't something extracted through fear –

Sarah Kelly –

Kelly It's freely given.

Gill lowers Deadsheep to her side.

Gill What more do you need me to give? (*Desperate.*)
I raised you –

Kelly You raised some wee girl in your head. You're
thinking of a picture of a child, hung on the wall of a house
no one lives in anymore. A place where any love that made
itself even slightly known, it was taken apart and debased.

Gill Not all of it.

Kelly Yes, all of it.

Gill No –

Kelly I'm saying look at me as I am, Gill. Love the me that
actually survived and I promise you, I will give you all the
love you want from me in return. Maybe that's what God
has been saying to you this whole time. This mirage of me
you keep chasing. This image of me that won't move on.
You need to cut it out of your mind so you can finally see
what's real.

*Gill lifts up her keys and feels the weight of them in her
hands.*

I'm ready.

*Gill looks at Kelly. She reaches out with her key fist and
hears Kelly's heartbeat. She slowly turns her key fist and
listens as Kelly's heart ruptures in her chest. And then,
with unearthly clarity, Gill hears Kelly's voice.*

Gill. Gill.

Gill (*softly*) Here I am.

*Gill takes her keys and uses the point of one of them to
rip Deadsheep apart. Kelly tries not to show how much
she is hurt by what she is seeing.*

Sarah Kelly –

Gill drops her keys and does the rest of the ripping with her hands. When she is finished she sighs deeply. The relief of this act is huge within her.

Kelly He loves us –

Sarah Darling.

Sarah reaches out to Kelly but Kelly shrugs her off.

Kelly (*doggedly*) He loves us. He loves us. (*Struggling.*) I'm trying to free you.

Gill numbly bundles the shredded Deadsheep she has in her hands and passes it to Kelly. Kelly shoves Gill and hits at her. Gill impassively holds Kelly's arms down at her side.

Gill (*softly*) There it is. There's what I put in you. My wee prizefighter. That's what's been missing.

Gill kisses Kelly's head. Kelly breaks free and violently pushes Gill away. She hits Gill. She hits her again. She stops. She breathes. She resets.

Kelly Sorry. Sorry. I. Sorry. I don't why. That's not me. I don't do that –

Sarah Kelly.

Kelly No, no, I really, let's just. Let's try again –

Sarah (*sharp*) Kelly. (*Beat.*) Leave us would you, I need to speak to your sister.

Kelly lingers.

Go on.

Kelly leaves without looking at Gill. Gill stands between Sarah and the exit.

Gill Here I am.

Sarah Here you are.

Gill You see that?

Sarah I did.

Beat.

Gill You said Come Home.

Sarah nods.

Why?

Sarah Why do you think?

Beat.

Gill To punish me.

Sarah Punish you?

Gill is nodding.

Gill (*pleading*) Yes.

Sarah What do you want me to do? Put you over my knee? We're two grown women.

Gill can't bear to hear this. She starts humming and shaking her head. Sarah looks up and sees the lights above them flicker and blare.

Gillian. Hai.

Sarah snaps her fingers.

Don't you go anywhere. You see me?

Gill nods.

You hear me? Listen to my voice.

Gill nods.

You remember that Colette? You and her were similar ages.

Gill nods.

Pretty girl. So pretty. Lovely tawny blonde wee thing. I was back in Belfast the other day, just shopping, and I saw her

there in the city centre. She was drinking. This is middle of
the day it is. Drinking. Being loud at people. People looking
at her. I saw her and I thought, I know that kind of day.

So I went over to her and I said, Colette, do you
remember me? It's Sarah. And she looked at me. And I was
ready for her to do whatever. Say whatever. That would
have been her right. But instead, she grabs me, and she
holds on to me, and she's crying. Shivering against me. She
felt like she was sheets of lightning. And that starts me off
so it does. The both of us. Outside Zara. Full waterworks.
For however long, I dunno, it could have been minutes,
could have been hours.

But then it ends, and she lets go of me, and she just slips
away. Danders off again like a wee animal on some route it
does every day. And I called after, but she wouldn't . . .
She just kept on wherever she was going, not looking back.
I suppose there was nothing more she wanted from me
than that.

Beat.

Gillian . . . I haven't stopped thinking about you. Not one
day of my life. Thinking about where you might be. What
you might be doing . . . I think . . . I was thinking this
place . . . It might be the place for you too. It's helped me,
it has, some of it –

Gill I'm not you –

Sarah No you're not.

Gill I can't be here –

Sarah No –

Gill I can't –

Sarah No. I see that now. (*Beat.*) I know, the choices I made,
it meant you had to spend a lot of time making up for where
I should have been but wasn't. I can see how that's spread
you out. But I'm here now. And I'm staying. So maybe you

can go find a bit of something that's just for you. (*Beat.*) And then come back and say hello from time to time.

Gill is shaking her head.

Maybe not. I'll leave that up to you.

Sarah smiles. She looks around.

(*Conspiratorially.*) I mean this sort of carry-on, it's not for everyone is it?

Gill laughs.

Gill That Richard fella . . .

Sarah Oh aye.

Gill Is he the absolute fucking danger I think he is?

Sarah Awk maybe. All these wee girls, they get locked in his orbit. And him, he acts oblivious . . . I don't know. But don't you worry about any of that. I've been practising every night. The speed I can move now he'll not even see the hand of me when it comes.

Gill She was talking about some teaching course . . .

Sarah Stranmillis.

Gill Aye. She was saying she wasn't sure . . .

Sarah Gillian, if I have to I will march that girl to Belfast at gunpoint.

Gill nods. She breathes in through her nose and catches a whiff of herself. She grimaces. Sarah leans in and sniffs her.

Ooft, that's rough. You want me to find you some clothes before you go?

Gill She brought me some earlier.

Sarah Grand. I'll leave you to it. Go check how she's doing. Probably in her room writing you a very determined email.

Gill Don't have email.

Sarah Sure that won't stop her.

Sarah picks up some of the fallen Deadsheep and walks to the door.

(*Leaving.*) Now. Somewhere in this place one of these fuckers is bound to have a needle and thread.

Sarah exits. When she knows she is alone, Gill goes to the page from Sarah she scrunched up and threw away. She smooths it out on the floor. She carefully folds it and puts it in the sports bag. She spots Kelly's phone has been left behind. She picks it up. She thinks to call after Sarah and then doesn't.
The white noise is still playing. Gill accesses the volume control for the speakers and uses it like Kelly showed her earlier. She turns it up all the way. She closes her eyes. The white noise becomes the noise of everything. Gill does not fight it.
Kelly enters. She is dressed as Gill wants to see her. Gill opens her eyes and sees Kelly. Kelly stands for a moment looking at her. She steps forward and takes the phone from Gill. The noise is so loud we might not be able to hear them.

Kelly Thank you.

Gill You came back.

Kelly Yes.

Gill smiles. Kelly points to the sports bag.

You've still not dressed?

Gill No. But I will. I promise.

Kelly Soon?

Gill Yes. Soon. I want to look good for you.

End.